Papier-mâché

fantastic step-by-step creations from papier-mâché

LORENZ BOOKS

This edition published by Lorenz Books
an imprint of Anness Publishing Limited
Hermes House, 88-89 Blackfriars Road, London SE1 8HA

A CIP catalogue record for this book is available from the British Library

ISBN 0-7548-0100-4

Publisher: Joanna Lorenz
Project Editor: Fiona Eaton
Designer: Lilian Lindblom
Illustrator: Anna Koska

Originally published as *30 Papier-mache Projects*

Printed and bound in Singapore

© Anness Publishing Limited 1997, 1999
1 3 5 7 9 10 8 6 4 2

CONTENTS

INTRODUCTION

If you've been in the habit of throwing newspapers away – even if you recycle them – think again. The thirty beautiful objects in this book are all made from newspaper and card (cardboard).

Papier-mâché made its debut in the seventeenth century, but reached its heyday in Victorian times when it was inlaid with mother-of-pearl, gilded, marbled, wood-grained and, most popular of all, lacquered in the Oriental style.

You can draw your own templates for the projects in this book, or scale up those provided by photocopying them or copying them on to graph paper. To do this, trace around the template, draw a squared grid over it and transfer the pattern, square by square, on to a sheet of graph paper with a larger grid.

Papier-mâché is easy to make and use; thin strips of newspaper are simply soaked in glue and then layered over a basic shape. Allow each layer to dry before adding the next one. For sculpted shapes, papier-mâché pulp is more effective. All you do is tear five sheets of newspaper into very small squares and place in an old saucepan with just enough water to cover. Simmer for 30 minutes. Spoon the mixture into a blender and blend to a pulp. Pour into a plastic container and add 5 dessertspoons of PVA (white) glue, 2 dessertspoons of wallpaper paste and 1 dessertspoon of oil. Stir thoroughly and the pulp is ready to use – just push it into shape with your hands. The quantities are ample for each project in this book, and if you store the pulp in an airtight container it will keep for several weeks.

When you have completed your papier-mâché structure, give it time to dry out thoroughly; this may take several days. A warm airing cupboard is a good place to leave things to dry. Once the papier-mâché is hard, you can smooth it with fine-grade sandpaper before priming it with white paint: use emulsion (flat latex) paint, undercoat or acrylic primer to hide the newsprint and provide a sound base coat for the final decoration. Once your project is painted and varnished, you'll be amazed at the way it combines lightness with strength, delicacy with sturdiness. It's hard to believe that such a variety of beautiful objects have their origin in such humble materials.

A Star for the Christmas Tree

Persuade the fairy to take a well-earned rest this year, and make this magnificent gold star to take pride of place at the top of the tree. The glittering relief design will glint subtly in the glow of the Christmas lights.

MATERIALS

pencil
corrugated cardboard
metal ruler
craft knife
cutting mat
newspaper
PVA (white) glue
paintbrush
gold spray paint
gold relief (puff) paint
gold glitter
thin gold braid

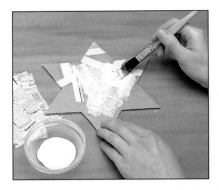

1 Draw the star on corrugated cardboard and cut it out using a metal ruler and craft knife. Always protect your work surface with a cutting mat. Tear the newspaper into thin strips and coat it thoroughly with PVA (white) glue, thinned with a little water. Work all over the star in a single layer. Allow to dry, then apply a second layer.

TIP

Brush the newspaper strips down with more glue as you apply them, to eliminate any bubbles of air. Work around the edges and points of the star neatly to keep the shape sharply defined.

2 If the star begins to buckle while drying, place it under a heavy weight. When completely dry, spray both sides gold and allow to dry.

3 Draw the design on one side in gold relief (puff) paint and sprinkle with glitter while it is still wet. Allow to dry completely before repeating the design on the other side. Attach thin gold braid with which to hang the star from the top of the tree.

LEAF CANDLE HOLDERS

*Make a stunning arrangement for the table by combining these bright
candle holders with sprays of real foliage. The freehand painted design,
with all the charm of folk art, is slightly distressed to give a mellow, worn
look. Several coats of acrylic gesso make a smooth porous surface which
takes the paint well.*

MATERIALS

tracing paper
pencil
card (cardboard) or paper for template
corrugated cardboard
cutting mat
craft knife
metal bottle cap
PVA (white) glue
kitchen knife
papier-mâché pulp
newspaper
wallpaper paste
paintbrush
acrylic gesso
acrylic paints
fine-grade sandpaper
wax polish
cloth

TIP
Use wax candle stickers to fix
the candles firmly in place if they
are not a perfect fit.

1 Scale up the template, transfer
to corrugated cardboard and cut
it out. Place the bottle cap in the
centre and draw around it. Cut out
the circle from the top layers of cardboard. Glue the cap in the hole.

2 Using a kitchen knife, build up
the leaf shape in papier-mâché
pulp to the top of the cap, sloping
down to the edges and creating a
ridge along each lobe. Allow to dry.

3 Cover with a single layer of
newspaper strips coated with
wallpaper paste. When it is dry,
apply three or four coats of acrylic
gesso, allowing to dry between coats.

4 Decorate with acrylic paints,
using alternate light and dark
tones. When dry, distress with fine
sandpaper. Apply wax polish and
buff with a cloth to a satin finish.

GRANDFATHER CLOCK

The grand scale of this project contrasts wittily with its unlikely paper origin to form a striking conversation piece.

MATERIALS

tracing paper
graph paper
pencil
scissors
card (cardboard) or paper for templates
cutting mat
craft knife
large sheets of corrugated cardboard
masking tape
newspaper
wallpaper paste
paintbrushes
thin plywood sheet
coping saw
drill
white emulsion (flat latex) paint
fine-grade sandpaper
acrylic or poster paints
varnish
clock movement, pendulum and hands

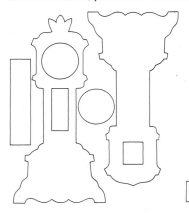

1 Scale up the shapes by photocopying them or copying them on to tracing paper, drawing a squared grid, then transferring them to graph paper square by square. Cut your templates and transfer to the cardboard sheets. Carefully cut out the pieces with a craft knife.

2 Use masking tape to assemble the front, back and sides. Fix extra pieces of corrugated cardboard inside the clock to strengthen it. Tape strips of corrugated cardboard around the sides, following the curves of the front and back edges, to complete the shape.

3 Cover the clock with a layer of newspaper strips coated with wallpaper paste. Draw a circle on thin plywood for the clock face: this should be slightly smaller than the front area it will sit on. Cut out with a coping saw and cover with a layer of papier-mâché. When dry, drill a hole in the centre to take the spindle. Fix the clock face on the front of the case with more papier-mâché strips, and continue covering the whole clock in papier-mâché until you have laid down a total of five layers.

4 Prime the clock with two coats of white matt emulsion (flat latex) paint, leaving to dry between coats. Form decorative details and numerals from papier-mâché and position them on the clock. When dry, sand smooth and apply another coat of white paint. Paint the clock using acrylic or poster paints. Allow to dry, then add a coat of varnish.

5 Cut out two cardboard hearts and tape them over the bob of the pendulum. Cover with a layer of papier-mâché and leave to dry, then prime with white matt emulsion (flat latex) paint. Decorate with acrylic or poster paint and add a coat of varnish. When dry, fit the clock movement, pendulum and hands.

STRING OF BOWS PICTURE FRAME

Inspired by a traditional kite-tail, this charming frame would make a lovely decoration in a child's bedroom, and looks equally pretty painted in bright primary or delicate pastel shades.

MATERIALS

cutting mat
metal ruler
craft knife
corrugated cardboard
paintbrushes
wallpaper paste
newspaper
scissors
PVA (white) glue
acrylic gesso
sponge
acrylic paints
string
matt varnish

1 Cut a frame and backing board from corrugated cardboard. Paint the two pieces with a good coat of wallpaper paste and leave to dry. This will prevent the frame from buckling later on.

2 Tear the newspaper into short strips. Dip them in the wallpaper paste and wrap around the frame to cover it completely. Allow to dry, then apply a second layer.

3 Cut eight 10 x 5 cm (4 x 2 in) strips of newspaper. Cover one side with wallpaper paste, fold the ends to the centre and pinch to form a bow. Fix a smaller, pasted strip around the middle of each bow and leave to dry.

4 Glue the backing board to the back of the frame, leaving the top open. Stick the bows on the frame and give the whole thing a coat of acrylic gesso. Allow to dry. Dip the sponge into pink paint and dab off the excess. Sponge the frame.

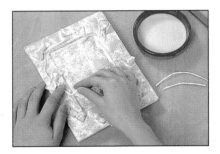

5 Cut short lengths of string and dip them into the PVA (white) glue. Arrange them between the bows. Paint the bows in assorted pastel colours and leave to dry. Give the whole frame a coat of matt varnish and allow to dry.

HEAVENLY BODIES MOBILE

Encourage imaginary adventures in space with this original decoration.
Printed with a map of the world, the globe-shaped paper lampshade makes
the perfect frame from which to hang glowing papier-mâché planets.

MATERIALS

4 balloons
newspaper
wallpaper paste
paintbrushes
scissors
thin card (cardboard)
ruler
masking tape
acrylic paints
glitter glue
galvanized wire
globe paper lampshade
round-nosed pliers
needle
fishing line

1 Blow up four small balloons to the size of your palm. Tear the newspaper into small strips and coat in wallpaper paste. Apply several layers of the pasted newspaper strips to each of the four balloons, ideally allowing each layer to dry completely before adding the next.

2 Cut a strip of thin card (cardboard) about 10 cm (4 in) wide and long enough to go around one of the balloons. Cut a row of curved rays along one long edge and a row of tabs along the other. Wrap the strip around the balloon, fixing the tabs down with tape. Cover the card with a layer of papier-mâché.

3 Paint this balloon red and yellow to look like the sun. Paint the remaining three balloons in bright, bold colours, allowing to dry before decorating with glitter glue. Carefully wind a long piece of galvanized wire around one of the planets to represent rings.

4 Thread two pieces of wire, each about 50 cm (20 in) long, through the globe lampshade to form a cross.

5 Using round-nosed pliers, form a hook at each end of the wires. Attach the sun and planets to the lampshade using a needle and fishing line.

GOTHIC STAR MIRROR

Painted in fresh pastel colours, this pretty little mirror frame has a simple relief decoration made with curly sausages of clay and naïve, freehand star shapes.

MATERIALS

pencil
thick card (cardboard)
cutting mat
craft knife
metal ruler
mirror
masking tape
short length of thin wire
newspaper
wallpaper paste
paintbrushes
white emulsion (flat latex) paint
self-hardening clay
modelling tool
acrylic paints
varnish

*T*IP
To make sure the frame is roughly symmetrical, fold a sheet of paper in half, draw a simple template and transfer it to the card (cardboard) before you cut.

1 Draw the shape of the frame on the card (cardboard) twice and cut out with a craft knife and metal ruler. Cut out the central shape from the front piece of the frame. Fix the mirror to this piece with masking tape. Make a hook from wire and fix it to the back section of the frame. Put the two pieces of card (cardboard) together, sandwiching the mirror between them, and tape securely.

2 Tear the newspaper into squares approximately 2.5 cm (1 in) across and use wallpaper paste to stick them in a single layer on both sides and around the edges of the frame. Leave to dry.

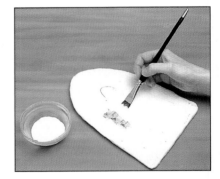

3 Prime with white emulsion (flat latex) paint and allow to dry. Roll some clay into long sausages and use to make an edging for the mirror and decorative scrolls and curls. Press on to the frame with the help of a modelling tool. Cut star shapes out of the clay and fix on. Leave to dry. Decorate with acrylic paints and varnish when dry.

BEAMING SUN WALL PLAQUE

*A cheerful sunny face looking down at you is sure to cheer you up, so hang this
wall plaque where it will do you most good – perhaps over the breakfast table!*

MATERIALS

pencil
pair of compasses
corrugated cardboard
scissors
PVA (white) glue
newspaper
paintbrushes
white undercoat paint
acrylic paints
matt varnish

1 Draw and cut five equal circles
of corrugated cardboard to size.
Glue three circles together. Bind the
edges with newspaper strips dipped
in PVA (white) glue.

2 Glue the remaining two circles
together and cut out a circle for
the sun's face from their centre. Trim
this smaller circle so that there will
be a gap all around it when you
replace it.

3 On the remaining outer ring
draw the rays of the sun and cut
them out. Bind all the edges, and
those of the small circle, with strips
of newspaper. Glue the face and rays
to the backing circle, centring the
face in the area left for it.

4 Draw the features freehand on
corrugated cardboard and cut
them out. Glue them on to the face.
Prime the whole plaque with white
undercoat and leave to dry.

5 Decorate the wall plaque with
acrylic paints. When dry, apply
two coats of matt varnish.

3-D HEARTS FRAME

*This chunky frame is constructed around a simple folded corrugated cardboard
base and decorated with heart motifs moulded from clay. Paint it in bright
colours to make the perfect setting for a picture of your favourite person.*

MATERIALS

*tracing paper
pencil
corrugated cardboard
cutting mat
metal ruler
craft knife
masking tape
wire
newspaper
wallpaper paste
paintbrushes
white emulsion (flat latex) paint
self-hardening clay
modelling tool
poster paints
varnish
PVA (white) glue*

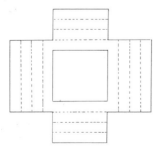

1 Scale up the template and
transfer it to the corrugated
cardboard. Cut out the frame, saving
the centre square. This will make the
backing for the frame. Score along
the dotted lines using a craft knife;
be careful not to cut right through.

3 Tear the newspaper into pieces
about 2.5 cm (1 in) square. Dip
in wallpaper paste and cover all sides
of the frame. When dry, prime with
two coats of white emulsion (flat
latex) paint. Leave to dry.

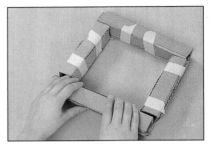

2 Fold each flap inwards along the
scored edges and fix together
with masking tape. Tape a piece of
wire to the back to make a hook.

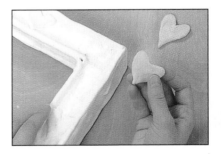

4 Form heart shapes by hand from
the clay and push them on to the
frame. Fix them in place by smooth-
ing down the sides of the hearts with
a modelling tool. Decorate the frame
with poster paints, leave to dry, then
varnish it. Stick a picture on the
backing corrugated cardboard set
aside in Step 1 and fix in place.

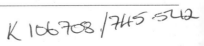

Deep Sea Mobile

Create a wonderful underwater world with larger-than-life marine
creatures in rich shades of turquoise, coral and blue.

MATERIALS

craft knife
3 blocks of florist's foam
corrugated cardboard
scissors
PVA (white) glue
newspaper
wallpaper paste
paintbrushes
masking tape
7 small brass curtain rings
string
papier-mâché pulp
white emulsion (flat latex) paint
acrylic paints
8 glass nuggets
gold paint
2 round beads
gloss varnish
galvanized wire
fishing line

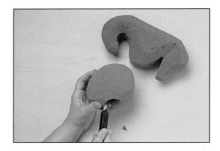

1 Carve one of the foam blocks into a sea-horse shape. Cut the remaining two blocks in half and carve four oval shapes to make the fishes. At one end of each block, carve out a mouth shape.

2 From the corrugated cardboard, cut out two side fins, one underside fin, one dorsal fin and one tail for each fish. Cut out a back fin, two side fins and a head for the sea-horse. Cut out a starfish shape.

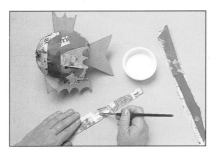

3 Cut slots in the foam and glue in the corrugated card pieces. Cover with papier-mâché.

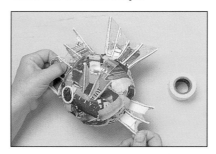

4 Tape a brass ring into each fish's dorsal fin and into the first curve of the sea-horse's back fin. Tape a ring on the end of a starfish arm and another on to the body directly opposite. Glue lengths of string along the fins and tails of the fishes and sea-horse, and around the eyes.

5 Cover the starfish shape with papier-mâché pulp and allow to dry. Cover all the creatures with another layer of newspaper strips, carefully covering the joins of the brass rings. Allow the pieces to dry, then prime them with white emulsion (flat latex) paint and let dry.

6 Paint the fishes blue with orange mouths. Leave the eyes white and glue on the glass nuggets. Paint the starfish in shades of orange and paint the sea-horse blue-green. Pick out the string details in gold. Stick the beads on to the sea-horse for eyes. Varnish all the sea creatures.

7 Join two 40 cm (16 in) lengths of wire in the centre to make a cross. Attach a 20 cm (8 in) length of fishing line to each end of the wire and tie to the brass ring on each fish. Use a longer length of line to hang the sea-horse from the centre of the cross. Use a shorter length to join the wire to the ring on the starfish body. Tie a length of line to the ring on the arm to hang the mobile.

SEASHELL MIRROR

Natural marine forms and curling waves influence this unusual mirror frame,
glowing with undersea colours and bejewelled with glass nuggets.

MATERIALS

tracing paper
pencil
card (cardboard) or paper for template
corrugated cardboard
cutting mat
craft knife
papier-mâché pulp
newspaper
wallpaper paste
paintbrushes
PVA (white) glue
white acrylic primer
glass nuggets
epoxy resin glue
gouache paints
gold paint
gloss and matt varnishes
mirror and fixing-tabs
plate-hanging fixture
screwdriver

1 Scale up the template, transfer it
to the corrugated cardboard
and cut out. Build up the three-
dimensional form of the frame using
papier-mâché pulp. Allow to dry.

2 Cover the whole frame with
several layers of newspaper strips
soaked in wallpaper paste. Allow
each layer to dry before applying the
next one.

3 Coat the papier-mâché with PVA
(white) glue and, when dry, add
a coat of primer. When it is dry,
attach the glass nuggets with epoxy
resin glue. Decorate the frame with
gouache paints and add extra detail
and interest with the gold paint.

4 Paint the frame with several
coats of varnish, using gloss in
some areas and matt in others to
provide contrast. Allow to dry.
Secure the mirror with mirror fixing-
tabs. Finally, attach the plate-hanging
fixture, securing all the screws with
epoxy resin glue.

EARRINGS & BROOCH SET

*This dazzling trio would make a jolly Christmas present. The earring
backs, brooch fastening and eye pins are known as "findings" and are
available from hobby and craft suppliers.*

MATERIALS

pencil
pair of compasses
corrugated cardboard
cutting mat
craft knife
newspaper
PVA (white) glue
fine-grade sandpaper
paintbrush
white and gold acrylic paints
strong, clear glue
glass "gems" and small beads
darning needle
9 eye pins
pair of earring backs
brooch fastening

TIP

If you prefer simple jewellery,
miss out the eye pins and
hanging beads for a more classic
look. The earrings and brooch
look just as good without them.

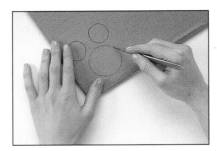

1 Draw two 2.5 cm (1 in) circles
and one 5 cm (2 in) circle on
corrugated cardboard, and cut out
with a craft knife.

2 Tear newspaper into thin strips.
Dip into diluted PVA (white)
glue and apply to the brooch and
earring pieces, overlapping them
slightly. Cover with four layers of
papier-mâché and leave to dry.

3 Smooth the jewellery pieces
lightly with sandpaper, then
prime with two coats of white paint.
When dry, decorate with two coats
of gold paint and then glue the glass
gems in place.

4 Make three holes along the base
of each piece with a needle. Fix
a hanging bead on to each eye pin,
glue around each hole and push the
pin into place. Glue on the earring
backs and brooch fastening.

GLOWING HEART WALL PLAQUE

This plaque couldn't be easier to make and paint: a bright, simple design will look best, and it will quickly be ready to enliven any bare corner.

MATERIALS

scissors
corrugated cardboard
strong, clear glue
masking tape
paintbrushes
PVA (white) glue
2 picture hangers
newspaper
fine-grade sandpaper
white emulsion (flat latex) paint
pencil
poster paints
gloss varnish
picture cord

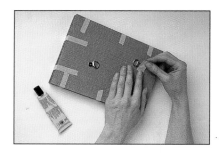

1 Cut three rectangular pieces of corrugated cardboard and stick together with clear glue. Secure with tape. Paint with diluted PVA (white) glue and allow to dry. Stick two picture hangers on the back with clear glue and secure with tape.

2 Soak small strips of newspaper in diluted PVA (white) glue and cover the plaque with five layers of papier-mâché, allowing each layer to dry before starting the next. Lightly sand the surface and apply two coats of white emulsion (flat latex) paint.

3 Draw your design and decorate the plaque with poster paints. Seal with two coats of gloss varnish. Attach a cord to the hangers on the back of the plaque.

Black Cat Bowl

The naïve charm of stencilling makes it an ideal style of decoration for papier-mâché ware like this bowl, which gains impact from the simplicity of the repeated design.

MATERIALS

bowl
petroleum jelly
newspaper
wallpaper paste
paintbrush
white emulsion (flat latex) paint
pencil
tracing paper
stencil card (cardboard)
cutting mat
craft knife
masking tape
black acrylic paint
stencil brush
gloss varnish

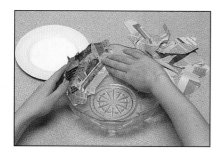

1 Coat the inside of the bowl mould with petroleum jelly. Tear the newspaper into strips, dip in wallpaper paste and line the bowl with six layers, allowing each layer to dry before applying the next one.

2 Remove from the mould. Trim the rim of the bowl with two more layers of newspaper strips. Allow to dry, paint with two coats of white emulsion (flat latex) paint and leave to dry again.

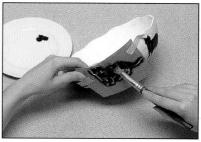

3 Transfer the cat template on to stencil card (cardboard) and cut out with a craft knife. Tape the stencil in place while you apply black paint with a stencil brush. When dry, apply two coats of varnish.

BAUBLE BOX

Make this box in any size you choose: you could fill it with handmade candies to make a lovely gift. It could be decorated in a variety of ways, perhaps with small pieces of brightly coloured pottery to emulate mosaic, or with glass "gems".

MATERIALS

heavy and thin corrugated cardboard
pair of compasses
pencil
cutting mat
craft knife
strong, clear glue
masking tape
newspaper
PVA (white) glue
fine-grade sandpaper
paintbrushes
white emulsion (flat latex) paint
poster paints
gloss varnish

1 From the heavy corrugated cardboard, cut two circles for the box base and lid and a smaller circle to create a lip under the lid. Cut the box wall so the corrugations are vertical; the strip should fit around the smaller circle. Using the template, cut the handle from the thin cardboard.

2 Gently bend the box wall at each corrugation to form a circle. Glue and tape it in position on the box base. Then glue and tape the lip to the underside of the lid and fix the handle in position.

3 Tear the newspaper into thin strips and soak in diluted PVA (white) glue. Cover the box and the lid with four layers of papier-mâché, keeping a smooth surface.

4 When the box is quite dry, lightly sand it, then prime it with two coats of white emulsion (flat latex) paint. Leave to dry. Decorate with poster paints, then varnish.

INCA MIRROR BOX

This exuberant flight of fancy is reminiscent of South American art. The arched recess is filled with three stylized sunflowers, and the same theme is repeated on the painted doors which open to reveal a small mirror.

MATERIALS

cutting mat
metal ruler
craft knife
corrugated cardboard
pencil
galvanized wire
masking tape
newspaper
PVA (white) glue
paintbrushes
white undercoat paint
gouache paints
gloss varnish
gold paint
epoxy resin glue
7.5 cm (3 in) square mirror
hinges

1 Cut out all the box pieces from corrugated cardboard. The arch-shaped back is 25 cm (10 in) high and 13 cm (5 in) wide at the base. The sides are 4 cm (1½ in) deep. Fix a shelf 13 cm (5 in) from the base and create a recess 4 cm (1½ in) deep and 7.5 cm (3 in) square for the mirror. For the frame around the mirror, cut a 13 cm (5 in) square and cut a 7 cm (2¾ in) square out of the middle: divide this in half to form the doors. Cut out the petals to go around the sides of the box. Cut out the three sunflowers and push them on to wire stems. Assemble the box using masking tape.

TIP

Make the middles of the sunflowers three-dimensional by gluing on scrunched-up balls of newspaper before covering them in layers of papier-mâché.

2 Cover the box, doors and sunflowers with several layers of thin newspaper strips soaked in PVA (white) glue. Allow each layer to dry. Paint with white undercoat and leave to dry.

3 Paint all the pieces. When dry, apply several coats of varnish. Add details in gold. Glue the mirror in the recess. Pierce three holes in the shelf and glue in the sunflowers. Glue the hinges and doors in position.

SUNBURST BOWL

This spectacular sun seems to burst out of the bowl towards you. This bowl is ideal for fruit, nuts or small display items, but you might well want to leave it empty to show off the design.

MATERIALS

petroleum jelly
bowl
newspaper
water
papier-mâché pulp
PVA (white) glue
paintbrushes
white undercoat paint
pair of compasses
pencil
gouache or acrylic paints
gold paint
fixative spray
gloss varnish

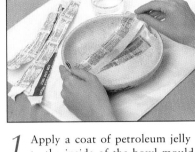

1 Apply a coat of petroleum jelly to the inside of the bowl mould. Tear some newspaper into strips, dip them in water and lay them over the inside of the mould.

2 Press the pulp into the mould in an even layer about 1 cm (½ in) thick. Leave to dry in a warm place such as an airing cupboard (this may take about five days).

3 Release the bowl from the mould and cover it in thin strips of newspaper dipped in diluted PVA (white) glue. Leave to dry.

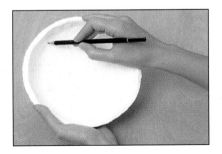

4 Give the bowl two coats of white undercoat. When this is dry, use the pair of compasses to position the sun shape accurately. Draw a small circle for the sun and a larger one to contain the rays. Draw the rays freehand.

5 Paint the bowl, filling in the yellow and gold areas first. Paint the rim in gold. Fill in the blue background, leaving a white band below the gold rim. Paint the outside of the bowl blue. Finally, paint the red border. When dry, seal the bowl with fixative and protect it with varnish.

STRIPED HANGING BOX

Make this bright wall container to cheer up a corner of the kitchen.
Its very simple design could easily be adapted to hold a variety of things.
Decorate it to suit your own colour scheme.

MATERIALS

tracing paper
card (cardboard) or paper for template
pencil
corrugated cardboard
cutting mat
craft knife
metal ruler
strong, clear glue
masking tape
newspaper
PVA (white) glue
fine-grade sandpaper
paintbrushes
white emulsion (flat latex) paint
poster paints
gloss varnish
picture hanger

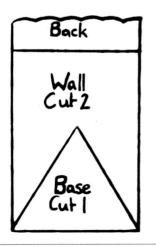

1 Scale up the templates and transfer to corrugated cardboard, remembering to make two side pieces. On a cutting mat to protect your work surface, cut out the pieces with a craft knife and metal ruler.

2 Glue and tape the pieces together. Tear newspaper into thin strips, dip into diluted PVA (white) glue, and cover the box with three layers of papier-mâché. You may not be able to cover the inside completely: go down as far as you can reach. Allow to dry.

3 Smooth the surface lightly with fine-grade sandpaper and prime with two coats of white emulsion (flat latex) paint. When dry, draw in your design in pencil.

4 Fill in the design with poster paint. Outline in black paint. Allow to dry, then seal with two coats of gloss varnish. Stick a picture hanger on the back using strong, clear glue.

DESIGNER BOWL

Small pieces of bright blue, yellow and orange paper have been used for this project, so that the papier-mâché itself creates the decorative impact of this striking bowl. Use a glass bowl for the mould, so you can see how the colours combine.

MATERIALS

glass bowl
petroleum jelly
coloured paper
PVA (white) glue
scissors
paintbrush

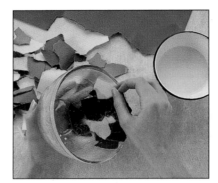

1 Coat the inside of the bowl with petroleum jelly. Tear the paper into 2.5 cm (1 in) squares. Soak a few pieces at a time, in assorted colours, in diluted PVA (white) glue. Press against the inside of the bowl, slightly overlapping. Cover the whole bowl. Add three or four more layers, allowing each layer to dry before adding the next one.

2 Leave to dry in a warm place – this may take two days in an airing cupboard. When the papier-mâché is thoroughly dry, remove from the mould.

3 Touch up the outside, if necessary, with more glue-soaked squares of paper and trim the top with scissors to leave a wavy edge. Leave to dry, then finish with a coat of diluted PVA (white) glue.

SUNFLOWER PITCHER

This pitcher looks like a modern Italian ceramic, with its elegant shape and brilliant colours. A sunflower moulded from papier-mâché pulp makes a sophisticated relief decoration.

MATERIALS

newspaper
wallpaper paste
1 inflated balloon
scissors
thin card (cardboard)
masking tape
round margarine container
fine string
papier-mâché pulp
paintbrushes
white emulsion (flat latex) paint
acrylic paints
gloss varnish

TIP
Make your own papier-mâché pulp following the instructions in the introduction. Make sure you mix it very thoroughly and once moulded into shape, allow several days for it to dry out (preferably in a warm place, such as an airing cupboard).

1 Soak strips of newspaper in wallpaper paste and cover the balloon with eight layers. Leave to dry. Cut a slit in the balloon and remove it. Cut a V-shape in the pitcher and tape a piece of card (cardboard) to it to form a spout.

3 To make the handle, roll up some glued newspaper, flatten and curve to fit the pitcher. Leave to dry. Cover with string, leaving 1–2.5 cm (½–1 in) at each end bare. Cut two slits and insert the handle.

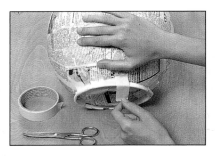

2 Use the cut-off rim of a round margarine container for the base. Bind it to the base of the pitcher with masking tape.

4 Use papier-mâché pulp to model sunflowers and leaves on the side of the pitcher. Leave to dry overnight. Prime the pitcher with white emulsion (flat latex) paint, then use acrylic paints for the background, flowers and details. Leave to dry. Finally, give the whole pitcher a coat of varnish.

DECORATIVE CUP

*Though you won't be able to drink from this Cubist-style cup, it makes
an original and amusing ornament.*

MATERIALS

*tracing paper
pencil
card (cardboard) or paper for template
corrugated cardboard
cutting mat
metal ruler
craft knife
PVA (white) glue
masking tape
paintbrushes
newspaper
fine-grade sandpaper
white emulsion (flat latex) paint
poster paints
gloss varnish*

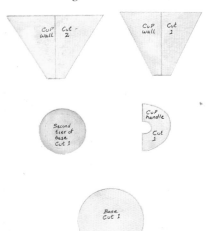

1 Scale up the template and transfer to corrugated cardboard. Cut out the pieces with a craft knife. Assemble the cup by sticking the three triangles together using PVA (white) glue. Strengthen with masking tape, then assemble the two base pieces.

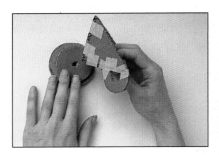

2 Stick the handle on one side of the cup and secure with tape. To stick the bowl to the base, make a hole in the centre of the base using a sharp pencil. Apply glue to the "point" of the bowl and fix this in the hole. Secure with tape.

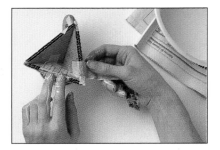

3 Paint the cup with diluted PVA (white) glue to stop it warping, then, using thin pieces of newspaper soaked in diluted glue, cover it with four layers of papier-mâché, allowing each layer to dry. Make sure the strips go neatly around the handle.

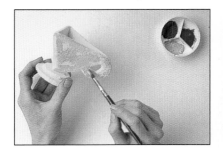

4 Leave the cup to dry in a warm place – about two days in an airing cupboard. Then lightly sand it down and prime with two coats of white emulsion (flat latex) paint. Decorate with poster paints. Finally, apply a coat of gloss varnish.

MIRRORED KEEPSAKE BOX

This mirror-decorated trinket box is an original idea for storing jewellery or other small objects. To break the mirror into fragments, put it between several thick sheets of newspaper and hit it with a hammer.

MATERIALS

pencil
section of cardboard poster tube
corrugated cardboard
scissors
masking tape
pair of compasses
PVA (white) glue
newspaper
4 marbles
wallpaper paste
epoxy resin glue
chemical metal filler
mirror fragments
paintbrushes
white acrylic primer
gouache paints
gloss varnish
gold enamel

1 Draw around the end of the tube on to the corrugated cardboard, cut out and tape to the tube. Cut out a slightly larger lid and another circle 1 cm (½ in) less in diameter. Glue together. Bend a roll of newspaper into a heart shape. Tape to the lid. Cover the marbles with tape.

2 Cover the box, lid and marbles with several layers of newspaper strips, soaked in wallpaper paste. When dry, glue the marbles to the box base with epoxy resin glue. Mix up the chemical metal filler, spread it on the lid, and carefully push in the mirror fragments.

3 Paint the box, not the mirror pieces, with PVA (white) glue. When it is dry, coat the box with acrylic primer. Decorate the box with gouache paints.

4 Coat the box and lid with several layers of gloss varnish and leave to dry. Add detail in gold enamel.

Art Deco Vase

This light, strong vase is not waterproof, but an arrangement of dried or artificial flowers would look very striking in it.

MATERIALS

tracing paper
pencil
card (cardboard) or paper for template
cutting mat
metal ruler
craft knife
corrugated cardboard
strong, clear glue
masking tape
paintbrushes
PVA (white) glue
newspaper
white emulsion (flat latex) paint
fine-grade sandpaper
gouache paints
varnish

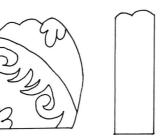

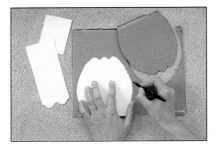

1 Scale up the template and use to cut out the vase shapes from corrugated cardboard – remember to cut two side pieces. Using strong, clear glue and masking tape, put the vase together, but do not attach the front section.

2 Coat all the pieces with diluted PVA (white) glue. Allow to dry. Soak newspaper strips in diluted PVA. Apply papier-mâché in four layers. Leave to dry. Give the inside two coats of white emulsion (flat latex) paint. Leave to dry.

3 Use strong, clear glue and masking tape to stick the front on to the vase. Cover the joins with four layers of papier-mâché. Leave to dry, then sand it down. Prime with two coats of white paint and again leave to dry.

4 Scale up the motif to fit the front and transfer it to the vase, outlining it lightly in pencil. Paint the vase and decorative motif with gouache paints. Leave to dry. Seal the vase with two coats of varnish.

PIGLET PUPPET

Children will love this cheerful piglet, whose head is quite easy to sculpt in
papier-mâché over a yogurt-pot armature (frame). You could make a whole
farmyard of animals in the same way.

MATERIALS
....

wire coat hanger
scissors
small plastic yogurt pot
masking tape
newspaper
thin card (cardboard)
PVA (white) glue
plastic-coated wire
paintbrushes
white emulsion (flat latex) paint
poster paints
fabric, 45 x 30 cm (18 x 12 in)

1 Untwist the coat hanger and straighten it out. Make a circular base at one
end of the wire. Bend the other end into a long hook. Make a hole in the
base of the yogurt pot and slide it down the wire until it is about 15 cm (6 in)
above the base. Secure with masking tape and stuff the pot with newspaper.

2 Tape strips of newspaper around
the pot to shape the head. Roll a
small strip of thin card (cardboard)
into a cylinder to form the piglet's
snout and tape on to the head.

3 Form cheeks with small balls of
newspaper and tape to the head.
Soak strips of newspaper in diluted
PVA (white) glue and wrap them
around the head. Build up four layers
of strips. Leave each layer to dry.

4 Cut two equal short lengths of
plastic-coated wire. Bind the
ends together with masking tape to
form trotters. Tape on to the wire
just beneath the head.

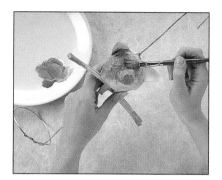

5 Cut out two ears from thin card (cardboard) and tape on to the head. Prime the head and trotters with white emulsion (flat latex) paint. When this is dry, paint the head and trotters a pink pig colour and add the features. Leave to dry.

6 To make the robe, fold the fabric in half and cut out the robe in one piece. Cut a hole in the fold line for the head. Spread glue along the edges of the fabric. Pull the robe over the pig's head and the sleeves over the arms, sticking down the edges.

Disco Doll

This spirited figure is formed from tightly taped and compacted newspaper twists.
The resulting structure is very sturdy – you can make quite large dolls and other
toys using the same method.

MATERIALS

newspaper
masking tape
scissors
PVA (white) glue
fine-grade sandpaper
paintbrushes
white emulsion (flat latex) paint
pencil
poster paints
black ink
gloss varnish

3 Tear newspaper into thin strips and soak in diluted PVA (white) glue. Cover the doll in four layers of papier-mâché. To make the hair, hands and feet, roll up small strips of glue-soaked paper between finger and thumb to form pellets of pulp and stick them in place. Paper over the pulp hair with short, thin strips of paper.

1 Twist a double large sheet of newspaper together to form a "rope" and tape the top, about 5 cm (2 in) down, to form the doll's head. Cut and shape the rest to form the body, and secure with masking tape.

4 Let the doll dry in a warm place. Lightly sand the surface and prime it with two coats of white emulsion (flat latex) paint.

2 Cover the body and head with strips of masking tape. Make the arms and legs, twisting smaller pieces of paper and taping them along their length. Cut to length, and tape to the doll's body.

5 When dry, draw the features in pencil and fill in with poster paints. Outline in black ink. Seal the doll with two coats of varnish.

SUNNY MOBILE

The smiling sun and fluffy clouds make a soothing arrangement for a nursery mobile, which will move gently if hung in an airy spot.

MATERIALS
....

tracing paper
pencil
card (cardboard) or paper for templates
thin card (cardboard)
scissors
5 eye pins
strong, clear glue
masking tape
newspaper
PVA (white) glue
fine-grade sandpaper
paintbrushes
white emulsion (flat latex) paint
poster paints
black ink (optional)
gloss varnish
thin florist's wire
fishing line

1 Scale up the templates and transfer to thin card (cardboard). Make four cloud shapes. Cut out the shapes and stick an eye pin to the centre top of each piece with strong, clear glue. Secure with masking tape.

2 Cover each card (cardboard) shape with three layers of papier-mâché, using thin strips of newspaper soaked in diluted PVA (white) glue. Allow the shapes to dry in a warm place before adding the next layer.

3 Lightly sand down each piece, then prime with two coats of white emulsion (flat latex) paint.

_4_ Draw the sun's features in
pencil, then decorate the shapes
with poster paints. Accentuate the
details with black ink if you wish.
When dry, seal with two coats of
gloss varnish. To assemble the
mobile, cut two 15 cm (6 in) pieces
of thin florist's wire. Suspend one
piece of wire from the centre of the
other. Attach the shapes to the wires
using short lengths of fishing line tied
through the eye pins. Attach a length
of line to the middle of the top wire
to hang up the mobile.

DAISY NECKLACE

Daisies and insects are always popular images with children, and they look really pretty on this simple necklace: perfect for any garden party.

MATERIALS

pencil
round object for tracing circles
corrugated cardboard
scissors
newspaper
PVA (white) glue
paintbrushes
white emulsion (flat latex) paint
acrylic paints
gloss varnish
darning needle
strong, clear glue
12 eye pins
coloured cord

TIP

You can use the basic idea to make a variety of necklaces. Simply paint the disks in a combination of colours for a more sophisticated look, or use triangles instead of circles for a modern geometric look.

1 Draw around a large coin or small round lid to make 12 corrugated cardboard disks. Cut them out.

3 Prime the disks with two coats of white emulsion (flat latex) paint and leave to dry. Draw a daisy or a ladybird (ladybug) on each disk. Fill in the designs with acrylic paints. Seal each disk with two coats of varnish and leave to dry.

2 Cover each disk with three layers of thin papier-mâché strips soaked in diluted PVA (white) glue. Leave them to dry overnight.

4 Make a hole in the top of each disk with a darning needle. Dab a little strong, clear glue over each hole and push in an eye pin. Cut a suitable length of coloured cord. Pass it through the eye pin of each disk and tie it before adding the next.

Puppet on a Stick

Papier-mâché has long been associated with puppet-making, as it is a cheap, lightweight alternative to wood or clay. This puppet is easy to handle, and its sumptuous costume can be made out of exotic fabric scraps.

MATERIALS

newspaper
masking tape
PVA (white) glue
fine-grade sandpaper
paintbrushes
white emulsion (flat latex) paint
pencil
poster paints
black ink
gloss varnish
2 pieces of dowelling rod, 10 cm (4 in),
30 cm (12 in)
fine string
strong, clear glue
scraps of fabric, torn or cut into strips

1 For the puppet's head, crumple a sheet of newspaper into a ball, then sculpt it with masking tape into the desired shape. Don't forget to make a neck, as the dowelling rod will be glued inside.

2 Soak newspaper strips in diluted PVA (white) glue. Cover the head with four layers. Squash strips of glue-soaked newspaper into pellets to make features. Fix in place. Cover with two layers of thin strips.

3 When dry, sand the head lightly and prime it with two coats of white emulsion (flat latex) paint. When dry again, draw in the features and decorate the head with poster paints, adding detail with black ink. Seal with two coats of varnish.

4 Tie the two pieces of dowelling rod together in a cross with fine string. Make a hole in the puppet's neck and glue in the longer length of rod. Leave to dry.

5 Tear or cut strips of fabric about 2.5 cm (1 in) wide and long enough to cover the dowelling rod. Tie the strips along the short crossbar that forms the puppet's arms. Tie some fabric around the puppet's neck to disguise the join.

SPOTTY DOG

*This eager dog is made from tightly rolled and twisted newspaper, which gives
a firm armature (frame) or support for papier-mâché. It might be fun to make a
whole collection of animals to go into a papier-mâché ark!*

MATERIALS

*newspaper
masking tape
ruler
scissors
PVA (white) glue
fine-grade sandpaper
paintbrushes
white emulsion (flat latex) paint
poster paints
gloss varnish*

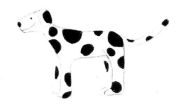

1 Take two sheets of newspaper and twist them tightly to form a "rope". Tape the ends of the rope, then bend it to form a fat rectangle about 15 cm (6 in) long, with one end extending about 5 cm (2 in). This end will form the dog's head. Tape the rectangle firmly in place.

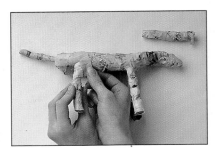

2 Using one sheet of newspaper, make a thinner rope and tape it along its length. Cut it into four pieces to make legs about 7–10 cm (3–4 in) long, and fix each one in place on the dog's body with masking tape. Make the ears and tail with small, thin rolls of paper.

3 Soak newspaper strips in diluted PVA (white) glue and cover the dog shape with three layers of papier-mâché. Leave it to dry completely in a warm place.

4 Sand the dog down lightly and prime it with two coats of white emulsion (flat latex) paint. Decorate the dog with poster paints, then seal with two coats of gloss varnish.

PIGGY BANK

*You won't find a friendlier pig to look after your pocket money! Sections of
an egg carton are the perfect shape to make his snout and feet.*

MATERIALS

*newspaper
PVA (white) glue
balloon
petroleum jelly
scissors
egg carton
masking tape
craft knife
paintbrushes
white emulsion (flat latex) paint
acrylic paints*

1 Tear the newspaper into thin strips and soak in diluted PVA (white) glue. Blow up the balloon and tie a knot in it. Cover with petroleum jelly or water and apply a layer of newspaper soaked in water, followed by five layers of papier-mâché. Leave the knot showing.

2 Once the papier-mâché is completely dry, burst the balloon and remove it. For the feet and snout, cut sections from the base of an egg carton and fix in place with masking tape.

3 Cut out triangles from the egg carton for the ears and attach them in place with masking tape. Use papier-mâché to cover the feet, snout and ears.

4 For the tail, roll up a piece of newspaper tightly and apply glue to secure it. Flatten the roll and wrap it around your finger to give it a coiled shape. Attach it with strips of papier-mâché. Leave to dry.

5 Cut out the money slot and prime the pig with two coats of white emulsion (flat latex) paint. When it is dry, paint the pig bright pink and add the features and decorations with acrylic paints.

ANIMAL BROOCHES

Animal designs always make good brooches; you could also make smaller versions
of these jolly creatures into matching earrings.

MATERIALS

tracing paper
pencil
card (cardboard) or paper for template
corrugated cardboard
scissors
newspaper
PVA (white) glue
fine-grade sandpaper
paintbrushes
white acrylic primer
acrylic paints
gloss varnish
brooch fastening
strong, clear glue

1 Scale up the templates and transfer the designs on to corrugated cardboard. Cut them out.

2 Soak thin strips of newspaper in diluted PVA (white) glue and cover the animal shapes with three layers of papier-mâché. Allow to dry thoroughly in a warm place.

3 Smooth the surface of the brooches with fine-grade sand-paper, then prime them and leave to dry. Add the features and decorative details with acrylic paint, then seal the brooches with two coats of gloss varnish. Leave to dry.

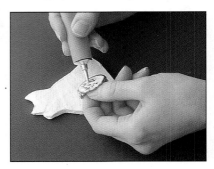

4 Attach brooch fastenings to the back of each brooch with strong, clear glue. Let the finished brooches dry in a warm place overnight before you wear them.

INDEX

Publisher's Acknowledgements:
The publisher would like to thank the following people for designing and
making the projects:
Contributors: Madeleine Adams, Petra
Boase, Amanda Blunden, Penny Boylan,
Annette Claxton, Ann Davies, Jenni
Dobson, Jan Eaton, Marion Elliot, Ariane
Gastambide, Anna Griffiths, Carole Hart,
Bridget Hinge, Rachel Howard, Labeena
Ishaque, Julie Johnson, Izzy Moreau,
Kim Rowley, Deborah Schneebeli-Morrell,
Jenni Stuart-Anderson, Pat Taylor,
Emma Whitfield, Josephine Whitfield,
Catherine Whitfield, Dorothy Wood
Photographers: James Duncan, John
Freeman, Michelle Garrett, Janine
Hosegood, Lucy Mason, Martin Norris,
Steve Tanner, Lucy Tizard, Shona Wood